The Storm Witch

Tapping into the Power of Storms for Transformation and Renewal

The Storm Witch: Tapping into the Power of Storms for
Transformation and Renewal

Copyright © 2023 Nichole Callaghan

Contents

The Calling of the Storm Witch

Since the beginning of time, we humans have marveled at the immense power of nature. The elements of earth, air, fire, and water each hold their unique allure. But there's something about the fierce combination of these elements during a storm that stirs a sense of awe and fear, mystery and exhilaration. This chapter beckons to those who are called to tap into this raw energy—the Storm Witches.

The Storm Witch

A Storm Witch is a practitioner of the magical arts who feels an intrinsic connection to the energy and power of storms. This witch taps into the primal forces unleashed during a storm, harnessing their transformative power. While all witches can use the energies of the natural world, the Storm Witch is unique. She aligns herself with the intensity, unpredictability, and fleeting yet profound impact of storms.

Storm Witches may specialize in different elements of storms. Some are drawn to the gusting winds that howl with voices of change. Others resonate with the torrential rains that cleanse and heal. The dramatic rumbling of thunder may speak to one Storm Witch, while the brilliant flash of lightning illuminates the path of another. Regardless of their particular affinity, all Storm Witches are united by their reverence for the storm's transformative power.

Ancient Connection Between Witches and Storms

In many ancient cultures, the storm was seen as a potent sign from the gods. In some societies, it was believed that witches and shamanic figures could communicate with these deities and, in some cases, even control the weather. The Norse god Thor wielded a hammer that created thunder and lightning, and he was often appeased by human intermediaries. In Ancient Greece, stormy seas were calmed by invoking the sea god Poseidon, again often through a dedicated intermediary.

Even today, folkloric tales from cultures around the world speak of witches who could summon rain, dispel clouds, or call down lightning. This link between witches and storms was usually tied to the community's need to regulate and understand the whims of nature. The Storm Witch, then, emerged as a powerful figure who could negotiate with the turbulent elements.

Symbolism of Storms

Storms are symbols of transformative change. They often arrive swiftly, drastically altering the environment before leaving behind a sense of calm and clarity. As such, storms symbolize various phases of life and experiences. They embody both destruction and creation. The destruction is often necessary to clear away the old, making way for the new.

Storms also symbolize emotional intensity. They often mirror our feelings of chaos, inner turmoil, or passionate fervor. Storms are therefore a metaphor for the emotional and psychological changes we undergo.

The Transformative Power of Storms

Storms have a profound transformative power. They alter landscapes, shift ecosystems, and force every living being to adapt. For the Storm Witch, this transformative power holds a deep spiritual significance. The storm acts as a conduit, connecting her to the divine, the natural world, and her own inner psyche.

Through their rituals and practices, Storm Witches seek to channel the storm's energy into personal transformation and renewal. By attuning themselves to the cycles of nature, they can encourage growth, initiate change, or seek healing.

Storm Witches, like storms themselves, are harbingers of transformation. They see the storm's power not as destructive but as a necessary part of the cycle of life. They acknowledge that without the storm, there can be no growth. Without the breaking down of the old, there can be no room for the new.

The calling of the Storm Witch is not for the faint-hearted. It requires courage, resilience, and a willingness to embrace profound change. However, for those who are called to this path, the rewards are equally immense. The Storm Witch does not merely weather the storm; she becomes the storm. In her hands, the storm's raw, chaotic energy is a tool for transformation, healing, and profound spiritual growth.

In the chapters that follow, you will learn how to tap into this powerful energy. You will discover the tools of the Storm Witch, explore the deities and spirits of the storm, and learn rituals and practices to harness the storm's transformative power. As you embark on this journey, remember the words of the poet William Arthur Ward, "The pessimist complains about the wind; the optimist expects it to change; the realist adjusts the sails." As a Storm Witch, you have the power to adjust your sails, to navigate through the storm, and to emerge transformed. Welcome to the path of the Storm Witch.

Recognizing Your Connection to Storms

Whether you've consciously acknowledged it or not, your relationship with storm energy is as old as your soul. Storms are a primal force of nature, one that is as deeply woven into the fabric of human existence as the blood coursing through our veins. Many people have a natural affinity for storm energy without realizing it, while others may feel an inexplicable pull towards the rolling thunder and the dark, swirling clouds. But recognizing this innate connection and understanding it is the first step on the path to harnessing the transformative power of storms.

When we talk about a connection to storm energy, we don't just mean a casual appreciation for a rainy day. We're referring to something far more profound, a primal resonance with the raw, wild power that storms represent. This might manifest as a sense of awe and excitement when a storm is brewing, or perhaps as a deeply rooted comfort when thunder rumbles across the sky.

To delve deeper into your personal connection with storm energy, it's essential to spend time in contemplation and reflection. Meditation is a powerful tool for this exploration, allowing you to quiet the mind and open the heart to your intuitive knowledge.

Before we embark on the guided meditation, ensure you are in a quiet, comfortable place where you will not be disturbed. Dress comfortably, disconnect any devices that might distract you, and take a few moments to settle into your space.

Guided Meditation

Start by closing your eyes and taking several deep breaths, filling your lungs completely and then gently exhaling. Picture yourself in your mind's eye as you are right now, sitting comfortably, feeling your connection to the earth beneath you, and the air around you.

Now, imagine that you are standing on a hilltop, overlooking a wide, open valley. You can see for miles around, and the view is spectacular. The sky overhead is clear and bright, with a few fluffy clouds drifting lazily across the blue expanse.

As you stand there, you feel a change in the air. A gust of wind brushes across your skin, carrying with it the scent of rain. You can feel a shift in the energy around you, a sense of anticipation that seems to electrify the air itself.

Turning your gaze to the horizon, you see a wall of dark clouds rolling in, gradually obscuring the bright blue sky. Lightning flashes within the cloud, briefly illuminating its towering structure, followed by the low rumble of distant thunder.

Notice how you feel as you watch the storm approach. Do you feel fear, excitement, awe, or perhaps a mixture of these emotions? Pay attention to these feelings, noting them without judgment. They are an integral part of your relationship with the storm.

As the storm gets closer, the wind picks up, whipping your hair around your face. The temperature drops slightly, and you can feel the electricity in the air, tingling on your skin.

When the first drops of rain fall, notice how you react. Do you welcome the rain, letting it wash over you, or do you seek shelter from it? Again, there are no right or wrong responses, just observe and accept whatever feelings arise.

As the storm rages around you, feel its energy. Feel the raw, wild power of the wind and rain, the crackling energy of the lightning, and the deep, resonating energy of the thunder. Acknowledge your connection to this powerful force of nature, accepting it as part of who you are.

As the storm starts to recede, leaving behind a world cleansed and renewed, reflect on your experience. What did you feel? What thoughts crossed your mind? Did you feel connected to the storm? Was there a moment of fear, awe, or perhaps a sense of peace?

Take a few moments to sit with your experience, absorbing the lessons and insights it offered. Remember, this is a personal journey, and your relationship with storm energy is unique to you.

It's not about comparing your experiences with others, but understanding your own innate connection to storms.

Understanding Your Reactions

The feelings you experience during storms provide important clues about your connection to storm energy. Excitement, fear, awe, peace - each of these reactions is a response to the storm's power, and understanding these reactions can help you tap into that power.

For example, if you find storms thrilling, you likely resonate with the transformative, high-energy aspect of storm energy. You might find storm energy helpful in driving change and progress in your life, breaking down obstacles and clearing the way for new growth.

If storms make you feel peaceful or comforted, you might resonate with the nurturing, renewing aspect of storm energy. After the storm, the world is cleansed and refreshed, ready for new beginnings. This can be a powerful energy to harness when you're looking for healing and renewal in your life.

Fear, while not a comfortable feeling, is also a valid and important reaction to storms. The power of storms can be frightening, but fear also represents respect and recognition of that power. If you fear storms, you might resonate with the protective aspect of storm energy, the power to shield and defend against harm.

Understanding your reactions to storms is the first step to harnessing their energy. Once you understand your connection to storms, you can start to work with storm energy in your rituals and meditations, using it to fuel your intentions and manifest your desires.

In the coming chapters, we'll explore various ways to work with storm energy, from storm-centered rituals to divination practices. But for now, take some time to reflect on your connection to storms. Journal about your experiences, noting any insights or ideas that come to you.

Remember, becoming a storm witch isn't about mastering a set of techniques or rituals. It's about forging a deep, personal connection with the power of storms, and using that connection to fuel your personal growth and transformation.

Elements of the Storm

Storms are an elemental wonder, a beautiful yet destructive dance between the raw forces of nature. As a Storm Witch, understanding and connecting with these elements is the heart of your practice. In this chapter, we will delve into the four primary elements of a storm: Rain, Wind, Thunder, and Lightning.

RAIN

Rain, in its most beautiful form, is life-giving water delivered from the heavens. It is renewal, the quenching of the earth's thirst, and the catalyst for the blossoming of life. In the realm of a storm, rain often signifies the release of built-up energy, washing away the old to make room for the new.

As a Storm Witch, the rain becomes a potent tool for healing and cleansing. A summer downpour can cleanse your body and spirit, washing away negativity and filling you with a sense of purity and renewal. Collect rainwater during a storm for use in spells and rituals; it can enhance any work related to healing, emotional balance, and transformative change.

Ritual: Rainwater Collection and Blessing

During a storm, place a clean, glass container outside with the intention of collecting rainwater for your magical workings. As you place the container, say the following:

Rain from above, as below,

Fill this vessel, let it overflow.

With each drop, cleanse and renew,

In this water, power accrue.

After collecting the rainwater, store it in a glass bottle and bless it with your intention:

Water of storm, of cloud and sea,

Empower my magic, so mote it be.

WIND

The Wind is the breath of the storm, carrying messages, spreading seeds, and changing the landscape as it moves. It symbolizes communication, change, and unseen forces.

Working with the wind can involve wind divination (also known as Aeromancy), using the wind's direction and intensity to uncover hidden truths. It can also involve harnessing the wind's power for spells related to change, movement, and transformation.

Ritual: Wind Whispers

On a stormy day, stand outside and let the wind envelop you. As it whirls around you, close your eyes and ask a question you seek answers for. Listen carefully as the wind whispers its responses. Once you've received your answer, thank the wind for its guidance:

Wind of storm, bearer of change,

Thank you for wisdom, vast and strange.

THUNDER

Thunder is the voice of the storm, a raw expression of power and strength. It symbolizes raw energy, power, and the disruptive forces necessary for profound change.

Listening to thunder can help you attune to your own inner power. It can serve as a reminder that even the most profound changes often begin with a single, disruptive act.

Ritual: Thunder Invocation

During a thunderstorm, safely indoors, meditate on the sound of thunder. With each rumble, visualize the power of the storm pulsing through you. Once you feel fully charged, speak the following:

Thunder's power, within me stay,

Guide my spirit, light my way.

LIGHTNING

Lightning is the illumination of the storm, the flash that reveals hidden truths and cuts through darkness. It represents inspiration, sudden insights, and drastic, quick changes.

As a Storm Witch, seeing lightning can be an omen of significant change or a sudden revelation coming your way. Harnessing the energy of lightning involves careful timing, strong intention, and respectful caution.

Ritual: Lightning Flash Inspiration

During a storm, watch for lightning from a safe place indoors. Each time lightning flashes, focus on an issue you need insight on. As the sky illuminates, visualize the light also illuminating your mind. After the storm, write down any insights you received, and say:

Flash of lightning, spark of thought,

Thank you for the insight brought.

As you develop a relationship with the elements of a storm, remember that respect for these powerful forces is paramount.

Like the storm, your practice is a dance between creation and destruction, healing and upheaval. Understanding the elements helps you navigate this dance with grace and power.

As we move forward, we will explore deeper aspects of the storm, from the spirits and deities that preside over storms to the tools and rituals that can enhance your storm witch practice.

But for now, take time to commune with the rain, wind, thunder, and lightning. Listen to their messages, harness their energy, and let the storm guide your transformation.

Storm Spirits and Deities

Across the tapestry of human belief, cultures have long associated the fury and beauty of storms with powerful deities and spirits. These celestial figures often serve as symbols of transformation, renewal, and the raw force of nature. Some are revered as gods of thunder, others as bringers of rain, and yet others as controllers of winds. This chapter will explore three such storm deities: Thor from Norse mythology, Zeus from Greek mythology, and Raijin from Japanese folklore. Each of these figures holds significant power within their cultural context and serves as a potential guide and ally for the Storm Witch. Let's embark on this journey of divine exploration, complete with simple rituals to help you connect with these deities.

Thor - The Thunderer

In Norse mythology, Thor, the son of Odin, is the god of thunder and lightning. He is often portrayed wielding his mighty hammer, Mjölnir, which he uses to shape the stormy skies. His chariot, drawn by goats, is said to cause the rumbling of thunder as it races across the heavens.

Thor embodies strength, protection, and steadfastness. He is the defender of the Aesir gods and humans against the chaotic forces of giants. As a Storm Witch, calling on Thor in your practice can help you tap into resilience in the face of adversity and harness the assertive energy of thunderstorms.

Thor's Offering Ritual

Begin this ritual during a thunderstorm if possible, to fully tap into Thor's energy.

Materials: A small hammer or representation of a hammer, a bowl of water (rainwater if available), and a candle (preferably red, the color of Thor).

Light the candle and place the hammer and the bowl of water in front of you.

Close your eyes and visualize Thor's chariot in the stormy skies. Feel the rumble of the thunder around you, resonating within you.

Say aloud, or in your mind, "Thor, Thunderer, I call upon your strength and protection. I offer this symbol of your mighty Mjölnir, and this water, reminiscent of your stormy skies. Stand with me, guide me, and lend me your resilience."

Leave the hammer and water on your altar or a special place overnight, allowing the energy of your offering to settle.

In the morning, pour the water outdoors as a final offering to Thor.

Zeus - The Sky Father

In Greek mythology, Zeus rules as the king of the gods from his throne on Mount Olympus. He is the god of the sky and thunder, wielding his thunderbolt with authority over the heavens and the earth.

Zeus symbolizes leadership, justice, and the power of transformation. His storms can be both creative and destructive, reflecting the transformative journey we often face in life. Invoking Zeus in your storm witch practice can help you embrace personal growth and exercise rightful authority over your life.

Zeus's Offering Ritual

For this ritual, gather a lightning bolt symbol (hand-drawn or otherwise), a bowl of olives or olive oil (sacred to Zeus), and a white candle (symbolizing the purity of the sky).

Light the candle and place the lightning bolt symbol and the bowl in front of you.

Visualize Zeus on his throne, surrounded by swirling storm clouds, his hand raised with a bolt of lightning.

Speak aloud or internally, "Zeus, Sky Father, I call upon your wisdom and justice. I offer this symbol of your mighty thunderbolt and these olives from your sacred tree. Guide me on my journey, help me to transform with the courage of your storms."

Leave your offerings in place overnight to allow Zeus's energy to infuse them.

Come morning, dispose of the olive offering outdoors as a tribute to Zeus.

Raijin - The Drumming God

Raijin is one of the most feared and revered deities in Japanese folklore. He is the god of lightning, thunder, and storms, often depicted surrounded by taiko drums, which he beats to create thunder.

Raijin embodies the chaotic and unpredictable aspects of storms but is also associated with fertility and agricultural abundance brought by the rain. Invoking Raijin in your storm witch practices can help you find peace amidst chaos and welcome unexpected changes with open arms.

Raijin's Offering Ritual

Prepare for this ritual with a small drum or drumming sound, a bowl of rice (a staple of Japanese agriculture), and a candle, preferably in a stormy blue shade.

Light your candle, placing your drum and bowl of rice before you.

Close your eyes and imagine Raijin amid the storm clouds, the sound of his drum echoing as thunder.

Say out loud or in your mind, "Raijin, Drummer of Storms, I call upon your dynamic spirit. I offer the beat of this drum in echo of your thunder and this rice, symbol of the abundance your rains bring. Help me thrive in the heart of the storm, and welcome the unexpected with courage."

Leave the drum and rice on your altar overnight to allow Raijin's energy to permeate.

In the morning, scatter the rice outdoors as your final offering to Raijin.

These rituals serve as starting points in connecting with these storm deities. As you grow in your practice, feel free to modify and expand upon these rituals as your personal relationship with these gods evolves. Through these practices, may you tap into the transformative power of storms and continue your path of self-discovery and renewal as a Storm Witch.

Tools of the Storm Witch

The essence of a Storm Witch is encapsulated not just within her connection to the elements and deities but also within the tools she employs. The tools of the Storm Witch are as dynamic and varied as the storms themselves, each holding its own energy and significance. This chapter will journey through some key instruments the Storm Witch might use, including jars of rainwater, wind chimes, and the profoundly powerful lightning-struck wood.

Jars of Rainwater

Rainwater is one of the purest forms of water you can find, untouched by human manipulation. Collecting and storing it allows the Storm Witch to capture the essence of the storm, its power, its purifying nature, and its life-giving energy. Rainwater can be used in a plethora of ways, from purifying and cleansing tools or oneself, to adding to potions, teas, and baths.

To capture rainwater, all you need is a clean jar or container with a wide mouth, and a clean cloth or filter to strain out any debris. Collect the rainwater during a storm, making sure to do it safely, especially during violent weather. Store the water in a cool, dark place, sealed to prevent evaporation or contamination.

Wind Chimes

Wind chimes serve as a bridge between the invisible force of the wind and the physical world. They make the movement of the wind audible, bringing the storm's voice into our homes and sacred spaces. Wind chimes can be used as a form of divination, to induce trance states, or simply as a call to the storm's energy.

Different materials produce different tones and carry various energies. Metal wind chimes, for instance, can bring sharpness and clarity of thought, while bamboo or wooden chimes might encourage growth and grounding.

Lightning-Struck Wood

Lightning-struck wood is an incredibly potent tool, carrying the raw energy of a storm within its charred remains. It is rare and can be challenging to find, but if you come across it, it's a treasure of immense power.

This wood has been forever altered by the force of the storm. It can be used as a wand, a talisman, or even a piece of altar decoration. It's especially effective for protection, transformation, and banishing work.

Other Tools

Other tools you might consider include feathers, to symbolize the air element and the wind's power; thunderstones, believed in folklore to be physical remnants of a lightning strike; storm clouds photographs or paintings, and recordings of storm sounds for use in meditation and journeying. The tools you choose are personal, and you should always follow your intuition when deciding what to incorporate into your practice.

Cleansing and Consecration Ritual

Once you've gathered your tools, it's essential to cleanse and consecrate them, imbuing them with your intent and clearing them of any lingering energies. This ritual can be performed during or after a storm to make use of the storm's purifying power.

Begin by gathering your tools and placing them in front of you. Light a white candle to symbolize purity and protection. If you've collected rainwater, have it within reach. If not, any purified water will do.

Take each tool in your hands one by one. Focus on the energy within it, visualize any negative or unwanted energy leaving the object. If you're comfortable, you can say something along the lines of, "I cleanse you with the power of the storm, and the purity of the rain."

Sprinkle some rainwater over the tool, visualizing it being washed clean. If you're working with a wind chime or another tool that isn't water-friendly, you can use a smudge stick or incense for this step instead.

Next, hold the tool up to the sky, or if indoors, visualize the stormy sky above you. Say, "I consecrate you with the power of the storm, by wind and rain, by thunder's roar, and lightning's flame. Be now a tool of magic, an instrument of the storm."

Feel the energy of the storm infuse the tool. Visualize it glowing with power, ready to aid you in your workings. Repeat this process with each tool.

Once you've consecrated all your tools, thank the storm and the elements for their aid. Say, "I thank the storm, the wind, the rain. In love and respect, till we meet again."

Remember, your tools are an extension of your intent and a bridge between you and the forces of nature. Treat them with respect, and they'll serve you well in your journey as a Storm Witch. Harness the storm's energy, let it guide you, transform you, and aid you in your magical workings.

Storm Divination

The storms, in all their majesty and power, are not just a spectacle of nature. They are carriers of messages and portents, imbued with divine energy. To a Storm Witch, the knowledge of storm divination is both an esoteric practice and a practical skill. By tapping into the deeper understanding of the clouds, winds, and atmospheric changes, you can predict the weather, gather insights into the future, and foster a deeper connection with the earth. In this chapter, we will explore two essential storm divination techniques: cloud reading, known as nephomancy, and baromancy, the divination using atmospheric pressure.

Let us begin our journey into the heart of the storm.

Nephomancy - Reading the Clouds

Nephomancy is an ancient form of divination that involves interpreting the shapes, movements, and colors of the clouds. Every cloud is a canvas that the divine paints with celestial brush strokes, each holding a message waiting to be understood.

To begin with nephomancy, first familiarize yourself with the scientific aspect of cloud formations. Understanding the types of clouds and the weather they typically foretell is paramount. Cumulus clouds, for instance, are the fluffy, white cotton-like formations that usually indicate good weather. In contrast, nimbostratus clouds, low, thick, and dark, often presage rain or snow.

Cloud Shapes and Figures

Once you've grasped the scientific knowledge, attune yourself to the more mystical side. Observe the clouds carefully, letting your intuition guide your vision. Do you see figures or symbols in the clouds? An animal, a plant, or perhaps an object? Like interpreting the shapes in tea leaves or candle wax, the images in the clouds can be deciphered using your personal symbol dictionary or traditional symbolism.

For example, seeing a bird-shaped cloud might suggest freedom or a forthcoming journey, whereas a tree-shaped cloud could symbolize growth or stability. As with all divination, the context and personal association play a significant role in the interpretation.

Cloud Colors and Movements

Pay attention to the cloud's colors. White clouds often carry positive messages and are generally a sign of peaceful weather. In contrast, gray or dark clouds may foretell a storm or difficulty. However, they can also signify the washing away of troubles or a period of intense transformation.

The movement of the clouds also carries messages. Fast-moving clouds might signal swift changes or turbulent times ahead, while slow-moving clouds could indicate a period of calm and stability.

Baromancy - Atmospheric Pressure Divination

Baromancy involves interpreting atmospheric pressure changes to predict the weather or divine future events. In this context, a barometer, an instrument for measuring atmospheric pressure, becomes a tool of divination.

Scientifically, high pressure typically indicates calm, sunny weather, while low pressure signals stormy weather. Pay attention to sudden changes: a rapid drop may mean a storm is imminent.

On a spiritual level, high pressure might symbolize a period of peace, joy, or productivity, while low pressure could indicate a time for introspection, self-care, or dealing with deep-seated issues. Rapid changes might foretell unexpected events or transformations. Remember, though, like stormy weather, these challenging times often lead to growth and renewal.

Meditation for Connecting with Incoming Weather

In addition to the above techniques, here's a meditation exercise to help you attune to the energy of the incoming weather:

Preparation: Find a quiet place outside where you can see the sky, preferably before a change in weather. Sit or stand comfortably. Ground and center yourself, feeling the connection to the earth below and the sky above.

Attunement: Close your eyes and take deep breaths, letting go of any distracting thoughts. Begin to attune your senses to the environment. Feel the wind on your skin, smell the air, listen to the sounds around you. Is there a storm brewing? Can you sense a shift in the wind or a change in temperature?

Visualization: In your mind's eye, visualize yourself merging with the atmosphere. Imagine yourself as part of the sky, feeling the ebb and flow of the air currents, the swirl of the clouds, the shifts in temperature and pressure. Ask the storm spirits or deities you work with to assist you in understanding the incoming weather's energy and what it signifies.

Receiving: Stay in this state of oneness with the atmosphere for a while, remaining receptive to any impressions, feelings, or thoughts that come to you. Do not force anything; let the atmosphere speak to you.

Return: When you feel it's time to finish, thank the storm spirits or deities, and imagine yourself gently separating from the sky, returning to your own body. Take a few deep breaths, feeling your feet on the ground. Open your eyes, and take a moment to adjust. You may want to drink some water or eat a small snack to help ground you.

Recording: Write down your experience in your storm witch's grimoire, including any impressions or messages you received about the incoming weather.

This meditation can help you develop a deeper connection with the weather and enhance your storm divination skills.

By learning to read the language of the storms, you're not only gaining a practical skill but also nurturing a profound connection with the storm energies. The clouds and winds become your allies, whispering secrets and guidance to those patient enough to listen. This sacred knowledge, once mastered, will empower you as a Storm Witch, allowing you to understand the rhythms of nature, anticipate changes, and navigate life with the wisdom of the storm.

Embracing the Storm Within

Every storm carries its energy, power, and potential for transformation. As a Storm Witch, learning to harness and work with these properties is key, not just in our outward rituals and workings, but also in the deep internal alchemy of the self. This chapter focuses on that inner journey, guiding you through the process of tapping into your own stormy potential, bringing forth change, personal growth, and self-discovery.

The Storm as a Metaphor for Personal Transformation

To start, it's essential to understand the storm's symbolic significance. A storm is not just a meteorological event; it's a metaphor for personal transformation and growth. When a storm approaches, it often brings unease and fear, just like the anticipation of significant change or the necessity to confront something within ourselves. Then the storm hits, bringing with it an outpouring of rain, the crackle of lightning, the roar of thunder - a whirlwind of energy that can feel chaotic and overwhelming. This is akin to the process of going through change or tackling internal conflicts. It's messy, intense, and sometimes scary.

But after every storm, there comes a moment of calm, a freshness in the air, a new perspective. This symbolizes the peace, growth, and understanding that comes after navigating the stormy seas of our internal world. As a Storm Witch, you learn to embody this process, becoming the storm, the change, and the renewal.

Embracing Your Inner Storm

First and foremost, embracing your inner storm requires acknowledgement and acceptance. We often try to suppress the stormy parts of our personality - our fears, anxieties, anger, sadness. However, these elements are as much a part of us as our joy, peace, and happiness. Like the thunder that rumbles within a storm, these emotions signal that a shift is needed. Pay attention to these internal cues.

Next, understand that just as every storm is unique, so is every individual's internal storm. Your journey won't look like anyone else's, and that's okay. There is no one-size-fits-all approach to personal growth and transformation. It's about finding what resonates with you, what helps you navigate your storm.

Guided Storm Meditation for Self-Discovery

Now, let's dive into a guided storm meditation designed to help you tap into your internal storm and foster self-discovery.

Find a comfortable, quiet space where you won't be disturbed.

Close your eyes and take several deep breaths, grounding yourself in the present moment.

Visualize yourself standing on a hilltop, looking out over a vast landscape. Dark clouds begin to gather in the distance. You can feel a cool breeze on your skin, carrying the scent of rain. Instead of fear, you feel a sense of anticipation.

As the storm approaches, instead of running or seeking shelter, you stand firm, ready to meet it head-on. The first drops of rain touch your skin. Let each drop represent a moment of self-discovery, a revelation about yourself that you've uncovered or need to uncover.

Lightning flashes across the sky, illuminating everything in stark relief. Let each bolt represent the sudden realizations or 'aha' moments in your life, the truths you have or need to acknowledge.

Thunder rolls across the landscape. Feel it resonate within you. Let each rumble represent your voice, your power, and your potential for change.

Stand in this storm, allowing it to wash over you, to transform you. Welcome the rain, the lightning, and the thunder.

As the storm passes, take note of how you feel. What did the raindrops reveal? What truths did the lightning illuminate? What did the thunder echo within you?

Take a few more deep breaths, then slowly open your eyes. Write down your experiences and insights.

Self-Blessing Storm Ritual

After you've engaged in self-discovery, it's time to bless and affirm the changes you're cultivating within yourself. For this, you'll need a bowl of rainwater (or tap water if rainwater is not available), a candle, and a journal and pen.

Begin by setting your space. Light your candle and place your bowl of water in front of you.

Dip your fingers into the water and touch your forehead, heart, and stomach, saying, "With the power of the storm, I bless my mind, my heart, and my will. May I be open to change, growth, and transformation."

Now, in your journal, write down the things you discovered during your storm meditation. These are the parts of yourself you are acknowledging and blessing.

Once you've finished writing, hold your hands over the bowl of water. Visualize stormy energy flowing from your hands and into the water, charging it with your intent for self-growth and transformation.

Now, with your charged water, anoint your forehead, heart, and stomach once more, saying, "With the power of the storm within me, I affirm my journey of self-discovery and transformation. I embrace my inner storm."

Extinguish the candle and close your ritual space.

Remember, the journey of embracing your inner storm is a continuous process. It's not something you achieve overnight. Every storm, every moment of introspection, every self-blessing brings you closer to becoming the Storm Witch you're meant to be – a powerful force of nature capable of profound transformation and renewal.

Storms of Change: Rituals for Life Transitions

The nature of life is constant change, and as Storm Witches, we align ourselves with the dynamic and transformative energy of storms to navigate these shifts. The beauty of storms is that they are transient, and they always bring change. They cleanse, revitalize, and leave the world renewed in their wake. As such, they are an apt metaphor and a potent ally for those undergoing life transitions.

Understanding the symbology of storms can empower us during times of change. The onset of a storm is a stirring of energy, a call to action; the climax of the storm represents the height of the challenge or struggle; and the aftermath of the storm stands for the resolution, the new beginning that follows upheaval. In this chapter, we'll delve into three rituals centered around these phases to aid you through significant life transitions: the Storm Call Ritual for the onset of change, the Eye of the Storm Ritual for enduring the height of transition, and the Aftermath Renewal Ritual for welcoming the new beginnings.

Storm Call Ritual

This ritual is designed to assist you at the beginning of a significant life change, whether it's a new job, a move to a new location, or the start of a fresh phase in life. You are standing at the precipice of a new journey, and the Storm Call Ritual is about invoking the storm's power to sweep away hesitation and fear, and to bring about the courage needed to initiate change.

Materials:

Storm Water (Rainwater collected during a storm)

A Feather

A piece of Aquamarine or Lapis Lazuli

A Blue or Gray Candle

Procedure:

Begin by cleansing your space and grounding yourself. Visualize the storm on the horizon, building in intensity. Feel the anticipation and excitement in the air.

Light the candle, symbolizing the spark of change. Say, "As this flame ignites, so does my journey begin. The storm brews at the horizon, the winds of change are stirring."

Hold the feather up high, calling upon the power of the Wind. Say, "Winds of the East, bringer of new beginnings, I call upon your power. Guide me on this new journey."

Take the storm water and sprinkle it around you, invoking the cleansing power of Rain. Say, "Rain of the West, cleanser and renewer, wash away my doubts, my fears. Make way for the new."

Finally, hold the aquamarine or lapis lazuli, crystals associated with water and powerful change. Say, "With this stone, I anchor my intention to navigate this change with courage and resilience."

Close the ritual by expressing gratitude for the storm's power. Let the candle burn out on its own if possible, symbolizing the initiation of change.

Eye of the Storm Ritual

The height of transition can often be overwhelming. When you're in the middle of moving homes, adapting to a new job, or navigating any considerable change, you may feel like you're caught in a wild tempest. The Eye of the Storm Ritual helps you find calm amidst the chaos, stability within the flux.

Materials:

A piece of Clear Quartz

A Purple or White Candle

A Bowl of Saltwater

A piece of paper and a pen

Procedure:

Start by cleansing your space and grounding yourself. Visualize being in the heart of the storm, with the world swirling around you. Yet within you, there's a calm and quiet center.

Light the candle, acknowledging the turmoil around you. Say, "In the eye of the storm, I stand firm. I embrace the chaos, for I know it leads to transformation."

Write down your current fears and challenges on the piece of paper. Fold it and place it in the bowl of saltwater, allowing your troubles to be 'storm-tossed.' Say, "Into the storm, I cast my worries. May they be dissolved in the tempest, and come out purified on the other side."

Hold the clear quartz, a crystal known for its amplification and clarifying properties. Say, "With this stone, I clear my mind. Amidst the tumult, I find my center. In the heart of change, I am tranquil."

End the ritual by offering thanks to the storm and the stability you've found within it. Let the candle burn out on its own, symbolizing your steady persistence amidst the ongoing changes.

Aftermath Renewal Ritual

After a storm, the world feels renewed. So too, after a major life change, we have the opportunity to start afresh. This ritual is to be done when you've navigated through the height of the transition and are ready to embrace the new beginnings that follow.

Materials:

Rosemary or Sage for Smudging

A piece of Sunstone or Citrine

A Green or Yellow Candle

A plant or seed

Procedure:

Begin by cleansing your space and grounding yourself. Picture the freshness of the world after a storm has passed—the clean air, the sun breaking through the clouds.

Light the candle, representing the light that follows darkness, the new beginning after the end. Say, "As the storm passes and the skies clear, I step into the light of a new dawn."

Hold the plant or seed, a symbol of new growth. If possible, plant it as a representation of your growth and renewal. Say, "As this seed (or plant) grows, so will I grow in this new phase of my life. From the storm's wake, new life springs forth."

Take the sunstone or citrine, stones associated with light, positivity, and new beginnings. Say, "With this stone, I welcome the light of fresh opportunities, new experiences, and renewed joy."

Close the ritual by expressing your gratitude for the storm's transformative power. Let the candle burn out, marking the beginning of your renewal.

Remember, transitions can be overwhelming, but they're also opportunities for incredible growth and renewal. As a Storm Witch, you have the power to harness the energy of the storm, using it to fuel your journey through these transitions, transforming them into experiences of empowerment and growth. Embrace the storm, and become the master of your own change.

The Healing Power of Storms

The raw, uncontained energy of a storm serves as a powerful conduit for both emotional and spiritual healing. We've explored the tempest's wrath and transformative vigor, but in this chapter, we delve into the calming aftermath and the therapeutic ambiance a storm leaves in its wake. We will explore the therapeutic potential that storm energy holds, and then I'll guide you through a storm meditation designed for healing and a storm bath ritual for cleansing and renewal.

Just as storms bring much-needed water to parched earth, they can also provide healing to our parched souls. They can cleanse us, help us grow, and give us strength. They can shake us up, yes, but sometimes that's exactly what we need to break free from the patterns and behaviors that are holding us back. To fully tap into the healing power of storms, we first need to understand the spiritual significance of storm elements and their relationship with our wellbeing.

Rain: Symbolically, rain is often associated with emotions and the subconscious. Its cleansing nature washes away the old, making way for the new. In the context of healing, rain can symbolize the release of pent-up emotions and the cleansing of negative energy.

Wind: Wind represents change and movement. It can blow away the metaphorical cobwebs, clearing your mind and spirit for new perspectives. In healing, wind signifies a refreshing change, a shift in old attitudes, or the removal of obstacles.

Thunder: Thunder embodies voice and expression. It's the sound of divine power echoing across the sky. For healing, thunder can symbolize finding one's voice and personal power, encouraging a loud, clear expression of truth.

Lightning: Lightning symbolizes illumination, divine inspiration, and sudden awareness. It lights up the path in front of us, even if just for a split second. In healing, lightning can represent powerful insights and epiphanies that radically shift our understanding and promote personal growth.

Now, let's channel these energies through a guided meditation and a storm bath ritual.

Storm Healing Meditation

Find a quiet space where you won't be disturbed. Sit comfortably, close your eyes, and take a few moments to breathe deeply and slowly, calming your mind and grounding yourself.

Visualize a storm building in the distance. See the dark clouds, feel the wind picking up. This is not a storm of fear, but a storm of healing and power. Feel a sense of anticipation and excitement as the storm approaches.

Visualize the rain starting to fall. Each drop washes away your pain, your worries, your negative thoughts and emotions. Feel them being cleansed from you, soaked up by the rain and carried down into the earth.

Feel the wind blow around you, sweeping away the last remnants of what you wish to let go. It brings change and a fresh start. Breathe in this clean, revitalizing air.

Now, hear the thunder. It is the sound of your voice, your truth. It echoes your strength and your power. Let it inspire you to express your feelings and stand up for what you believe in.

Lastly, visualize the lightning. With each flash, gain insights and ideas. See your path forward lit up in front of you. This is your time to shine.

As the storm fades, visualize the calm and clarity it leaves behind. You have been cleansed and healed, changed, and empowered. Carry this feeling with you as you slowly bring your awareness back to your surroundings.

Storm Bath Ritual

Draw a warm bath and add sea salts, which are known for their cleansing properties. As the bath fills, gather storm-charged items such as a jar of rainwater, a wind chime, or a piece of fulgurite.

Before entering the bath, take a moment to center yourself. Hold each storm-charged item, feeling its energy and the power of the storm that charged it.

Step into the bath, immersing yourself in the water. Close your eyes and visualize a storm surrounding you. Feel the rain cleansing you, the wind refreshing you, the thunder empowering you, and the lightning enlightening you.

Remain in the bath for as long as feels right, continuing to visualize the storm and its healing effects.

When you're ready, let the water drain away, imagining it carrying away any remaining negativity or pain.

Dry yourself and thank the storm energies for their healing. Carry this sense of renewal with you, reminding yourself of your cleansing whenever you need a boost of healing energy.

Through this exploration of the healing power of storms, we can find a balance between the turmoil and tranquility, the chaos and the calm.

A storm witch learns not only to endure the tempest but to thrive within it, drawing upon its powerful energy for profound emotional and spiritual healing.

By embracing the storm, we harness its power to cleanse, renew, and ultimately, transform.

The Wrath of the Storm: Protection and Banishing

Life, as we know it, is a complex web of energies interacting in harmony or discord. As a Storm Witch, you've begun to understand and harness the tumultuous energy of the storm. Now, it's time to explore its protective potential, to learn how to utilize its wrath to your advantage. This chapter focuses on protection and banishing. It will introduce you to the storm protection charm and the thunder banishing ritual, two powerful practices that can shield you from harmful energies and remove unwanted influences from your life.

Protection, in a witch's world, is not about building impenetrable walls, but about grounding and harmonizing with the energies around us. It's about invoking power from within to create a safe space, a sanctuary amidst the tempest of life. Similarly, banishing is not about aggression or violence, but rather about transformation and transmutation—taking an unwanted, negative energy and converting it into something positive.

Storm Protection Charm

The storm protection charm is an amulet that harnesses the shielding energies of the storm to protect you from harm and negativity. It's a simple, yet potent, tool that can be crafted from readily available materials.

Materials:

A small glass bottle or jar

Rainwater from a thunderstorm

Lightning-struck wood, or regular wood with a sigil of a lightning bolt drawn on it

Black tourmaline or any protective stone

Feathers from a bird associated with storms (ethically sourced)

Blue or black ribbon

Begin by cleansing your materials. You may do this by smudging with sage or by holding them in the smoke from an incense stick. Visualize any residual energy being carried away on the smoke.

Pour the rainwater into the jar, saying, "Rain of the storm, lend your protection. Create a barrier, a reflection."

Add the piece of lightning-struck wood or wood with a lightning sigil. As you do, say, "Bolt of lightning, grant your might. Energize this charm, ignite."

Now, add the black tourmaline, saying, "Stone of power, imbue this charm. Safeguard me, keep me from harm."

Finally, add the storm bird feather. As you place it in the bottle, say, "Feather of flight, imbue with your grace. Shield me from negativity, in every place."

Seal the bottle and tie the ribbon around its neck. As you tie the ribbon, visualize it forming a protective barrier around you.

To activate the charm, hold it in your hands during a storm, allowing it to absorb the energy. Visualize the storm imbuing the charm with its protective power.

Remember, the words you use, while provided here, can be modified to fit your personal feelings and intentions. What's crucial is the intention you put behind the words, the energy you channel into the charm.

Thunder Banishing Ritual

Storms are a force of change and transformation. They can uproot trees, reshape landscapes, and cleanse the air. A thunder banishing ritual draws upon this transformative power to help you banish unwanted influences from your life, whether they be habits, relationships, or energies.

Materials:

A black candle

A piece of paper and a pen

A cauldron or fire-proof container

Rainwater (preferably from a thunderstorm)

Begin the ritual during a thunderstorm. The rumbling thunder and flashes of lightning will enhance the potency of your working.

Light the black candle, focusing on the flame. Visualize the storm's energy being drawn into the candle's light.

Write what you wish to banish on the piece of paper. This could be a habit, a person, a situation, or even an aspect of yourself that you want to change. As you write, imagine the storm's power charging your intention.

Once you have finished writing, say aloud: "By the thunder's roar, by lightning's strike, I banish thee from my life. In the storm's transformative might, you no longer have a place or right."

Burn the paper in the flame of the black candle. As it catches fire, visualize the unwanted influence being consumed by the storm, transformed, and banished by its power.

Once the paper is reduced to ashes, extinguish the flame with rainwater. As you pour the water, say: "With this storm water, I cleanse and restore. What once was, is no more."

Safely dispose of the ashes outside, returning them to nature. As you do, imagine any lingering remnants of the unwanted influence being carried away by the wind.

Protection and banishing rituals, like these, are cornerstones of storm witchery. They enable us to weather life's trials, helping us create safe spaces where we can grow and transform. The storm is not just a destructive force, but a protective and transformative one as well. By understanding this dual nature, we can more effectively harness the storm's energy and tap into its profound magic.

Storms of Love: Rituals for Relationships

The energy of a storm, wild and passionate, mirrors the depth and intensity of human relationships. Storms can unleash torrential rains, representing emotions that flow freely and nurture the earth, or violent winds, reflecting tumultuous times that test the bonds between individuals. These forces are not to be feared but harnessed and respected. They are the bedrock of the Storm Witch's practice.

In this chapter, we will explore how to use storm energy to enhance and mend relationships, including romantic connections and friendships. We will delve into two powerful rituals: the Lovers' Storm Dance Ritual, designed for couples, and the Friendship Rain Blessing, a ritual designed to solidify and bless platonic relationships.

The Lovers' Storm Dance Ritual

Just as two storm fronts can merge to create a more significant, more powerful storm, two people can join their energies in a bond that transforms their individual selves. The Lovers' Storm Dance Ritual allows a couple to express their love and commitment in the presence of the storm's vibrant energy.

Materials Needed:

A quiet, safe outdoor space during a storm (If it is not safe to be outside during the storm, adapt the ritual for an indoor setting, using the sound of the storm from an open window.)

Two blue candles

Rainwater collected from a past storm

A piece of paper and a pen for each person

Steps:

Stand facing each other in your chosen space, hands clasped. Each person should have their candle, paper, and pen.

Take a moment to breathe in the energy of the storm, letting its strength fill you. Speak your partner's name, and let them do the same.

On your pieces of paper, write down your hopes and dreams for the relationship. These can include shared goals, personal growth you hope to achieve together, or ways you wish to support each other.

Exchange papers and read what your partner has written. Take a moment to reflect on these shared dreams and how they resonate with your feelings.

Together, light the candles. As the flames flicker, imagine your individual energies, like two storm fronts, merging into a single, powerful entity.

Holding the papers over the candles, allow them to catch fire (safety first!), then place them in a fire-safe dish. As they burn, imagine any barriers between you being broken down, just like the storm breaks down barriers in nature.

Once the papers have turned to ash, mix the ashes with the collected rainwater. This creates a physical symbol of your combined hopes, dreams, and energies.

Beginning a slow, deliberate dance, take turns sprinkling the ash-infused water on each other. This act is a blessing, a way of physically imbuing your partner with the energy of your shared dreams.

Close the ritual by expressing your love for each other, spoken from the heart. Remember, it's not the words that matter most but the sincerity behind them.

Extinguish the candles and thank the storm for its energy. Stay in each other's arms until the storm subsides, symbolizing the tranquility that can exist even after the most intense expressions of emotion.

The Friendship Rain Blessing

Friendships, like storms, can bring refreshment and life-giving energy. They are relationships that can persist through the calm and through the storm. This ritual is intended to deepen existing friendships and bless them with the renewing energy of rain.

Materials Needed:

A comfortable outdoor space where you can sit during a rainstorm

A glass or chalice for each person

A friendship charm or token for each person

Steps:

Sit together in your chosen space, each with a glass or chalice in front of you. Have the friendship charms or tokens at hand.

As the rain begins to fall, allow the glasses to fill naturally. This is an opportunity to share thoughts, dreams, and laughter.

Once the glasses have collected enough rainwater, each person should take their friendship token and, while holding it, share a cherished memory of the other person or express what the friendship means to them.

Next, drop the token into the rain-filled chalice, symbolizing your shared experiences being nurtured by the rain's renewing energy.

Now, each person picks up their chalice, holds it up to the rain, and says, "May the energy of the storm bless our bond, as the rain nurtures the earth."

Pour out a little rainwater from each chalice onto the earth, symbolizing your wish for your friendship to continue to grow and flourish.

Close the ritual by thanking the storm and the rain for their blessings. Each person should then take their friendship token and keep it somewhere safe as a reminder of the bond shared and the blessing given.

Remember, rituals are a tool for focusing your intention and energy. These rituals are just a starting point; feel free to adapt them to fit your relationships and personal practice. In the end, it's the intention and the connection that count. Harness the storm's energy to nurture your relationships, and let the transformative power of nature guide your path.

Cultivating the Storm: Weather Working

The practice of Weather Working is as old as humanity itself. Ancient cultures saw the weather as an integral part of their life and existence, and they developed methods of interaction and manipulation that we now understand as the rudiments of weather magic. They begged for rain to quench dry lands, sought winds to guide their ships, and implored the skies for benevolence. As a Storm Witch, you are the modern embodiment of this ancient tradition.

Weather Working is a complex practice. It's about more than merely casting a spell or performing a ritual to influence meteorological patterns. It is about understanding the climate, respecting its power, and connecting to its energy on a deep, intimate level. It is about establishing a bond with the elements of a storm and weaving their magic into your life. Before we dive into this, let's examine the ethics involved.

Weather Working Ethics

Ethics play a crucial role in any form of witchcraft, and Weather Working is no exception. It is essential to approach weather magic with respect and responsibility. Understand that while you might desire a particular weather outcome, your desires may not be in alignment with the needs of the local ecosystem, animals, plants, or even other humans.

Therefore, when practicing weather magic, remember these key ethical points:

Do No Harm: Always ensure your actions are not detrimental to the environment or others. For instance, summoning a severe storm might cause damage to property and wildlife, or even endanger lives.

Respect Nature: Understand and respect the natural cycles of the weather. Extreme weather events, like storms, play crucial roles in maintaining the earth's balance. Seek to work with these cycles rather than against them.

Permission: When practicing weather magic in communal areas or affecting areas beyond your own property, seek permission from the spirits of the land, other residents, or your deities, if applicable.

The Ritual of Calling Rain

The ritual of calling rain is a practice that requires the utmost respect for water and its life-giving properties. Before you begin, ensure you're clear about your intentions and the need for rain is genuine and ethical. This is not a ritual to be used for personal gain but rather a tool for harmony with the weather and the land.

Materials:

A blue candle to symbolize water and rain.

A bowl of fresh water.

A piece of aquamarine or other water-associated crystal.

Rainwater incense or any earthy incense.

Procedure:

Begin by grounding yourself. Take deep, slow breaths, visualizing your energy connecting with the earth beneath you.

Light the blue candle and the incense, saying, "By the power of the water and earth, I invoke the spirits of the rain."

Take the bowl of water in your hands. Visualize the water in the bowl as the clouds in the sky, heavy with moisture. Feel the coolness of the water and imagine it falling as rain on the land.

Hold the aquamarine, feeling its energy. Aquamarine is a stone of the sea, with strong connections to water and rain. Ask the stone to lend its energy to your ritual.

Repeat the following chant:

"Clouds gather, waters descend,

Quench the earth, let the dry spell end.

Blessings pour from the sky above,

Bring us rain, with peace and love."

Repeat this chant as many times as you feel necessary, visualizing the rain falling and replenishing the earth.

When you feel the ritual is complete, thank the spirits of the rain and the water. Extinguish the candle and incense.

Leave the bowl of water outside under the sky if possible, as an offering and a beacon for the rain you seek. The energy of the ritual remains, and it will help guide the rain to your location.

Meditation for Calming Stormy Weather

At times, stormy weather can become intense and possibly threatening. In these situations, a calming meditation can help soothe tumultuous energy. Before you begin, make sure your intentions are clear and ethical. Do not attempt to stop a necessary natural event, only to mitigate potential harm.

Procedure:

Find a quiet place where you will not be disturbed. Sit comfortably and close your eyes.

Start by grounding yourself. Visualize roots extending from your body into the earth, anchoring you firmly to the ground.

Imagine your energy extending upwards into the stormy sky, reaching the heart of the storm. Visualize the swirling dark clouds, the flashes of lightning, and the pouring rain.

Begin to send calming energy into the storm. Visualize this energy as a soft, soothing light, gently seeping into the storm and quietening its turmoil.

As you breathe, visualize the storm's energy harmonizing with yours, the severe weather gradually subsiding, the clouds lightening, and the rain slowing.

Repeat this calming affirmation: "I call upon the forces of nature, harmonize, and calm. Let peace return to the land under the storm's gentle palm."

Continue this meditation until you feel a sense of peace and calm. When you finish, visualize your energy gently retracting back into your body, leaving a sense of tranquility in the storm.

Slowly open your eyes and ground yourself again. Remember to thank the storm for its understanding and cooperation.

Remember, these practices should be done with respect, wisdom, and caution. You are working with powerful forces. While Weather Working is part of the Storm Witch's path, it is essential to acknowledge the responsibility that comes with such practices. Enjoy the storm's energy, revel in its power, but always remember to walk this path with respect and love for the incredible forces you are privileged to work with.

Storms and the Seasons: Sabbat Celebrations

As we journey through the Wheel of the Year, we come across eight Sabbats: Yule, Imbolc, Ostara, Beltane, Litha, Lammas, Mabon, and Samhain. Each has its own unique energy, and each offers a unique opportunity to connect with the energy of storms. In this chapter, we will explore ways to incorporate storm symbolism and energy into your rituals and celebrations of each Sabbat.

Yule (Winter Solstice)

The longest night of the year, Yule symbolizes the triumph of light over darkness. The storm at Yule is a reflection of the dark before the dawn, the tension before the release, the potential energy before the transformation. To honor the storm energy during Yule, you may consider performing the Ritual of the Winter Storm.

The Ritual of the Winter Storm:

Prepare your space by setting up an altar with representations of storm energy, such as a bowl of snow or ice, a feather to symbolize wind, and a candle for fire. Begin by lighting the candle and saying, "In the deepest dark, the spark of transformation flickers." Hold the feather and say, "Wind of winter, bring change and renewal." Hold the snow or ice and say, "The icy storm cleanses and purifies." Spend a moment in meditation, visualizing a winter storm and its transformative energy. Finally, extinguish the candle, signifying the transformation from dark to light.

Imbolc

Imbolc is the celebration of the first signs of spring, the return of the light, and the initial stirrings of life beneath the frozen ground. Storms at this time often bring the last snow of the season, a final cleansing before the emergence of new life.

Imbolc Rain Ritual:

Set your altar with a white candle and a bowl of melted snow or rainwater. Light the candle, representing the returning light, and say, "As the light returns, so does life." Pour the water into a pot of soil as you visualize a nourishing rain feeding the seeds beneath the ground. Say, "Storms of Imbolc, nourish the earth. Prepare for the new life to come."

Ostara (Spring Equinox)

Ostara represents the balance of light and darkness, the tipping point when the light finally outweighs the dark. Spring storms at Ostara are usually vibrant and refreshing, often bringing the necessary showers that truly awaken the earth from its winter slumber.

Spring Storm Dance:

For Ostara, consider an outdoor ritual if the weather and your circumstances permit. Begin by grounding yourself barefoot on the earth. Feel the connection to the ground, the energy pulsing below. Raise your arms to the sky, feel the air swirling around you, the potential energy of the coming storm. Begin to move, to sway, to dance. As you dance, visualize the spring storm: the thunder echoing the heartbeat of the earth, the lightning illuminating the world, the rain bringing life-giving water to the waking plants. Welcome the storm, welcome the balance it brings, and welcome the new life it nurtures.

Beltane

Beltane is a celebration of fertility, abundance, and the blossoming of life. The storms of this time are often robust, filled with thunder and lightning, mirroring the vivacious life force burgeoning on earth.

Beltane Thunder Ritual:

In preparation, gather thunderwater (rainwater collected during a thunderstorm) and a drum or a noise-making instrument. At your altar, light a green candle, symbolizing life and abundance. Play your drum or instrument, emulating the sound of thunder, and say, "As the thunder shakes the skies, so does life force quake within all beings." Sprinkle the thunderwater around your space, saying, "May the fertile rains of Beltane bless and nourish."

Litha (Summer Solstice)

Litha is the peak of light, the longest day, a time of joy and celebration. Summer storms, much like the season, are full of power and light, often arriving with little warning and departing just as swiftly, leaving refreshed earth in their wake.

Litha Lightning Ritual:

Prepare your altar with a gold or yellow candle and a piece of fulgurite, if available, or another stone associated with storms. As you light the candle, say, "The light is at its peak, the power of the sun at its mightiest." Hold your stone and visualize a summer storm, focusing particularly on the flashes of lightning, embodying the power and suddenness of transformation. Say, "As lightning transforms, so shall my path."

Lammas

Lammas is the time of the first harvest, the beginning of reaping what has been sown. The storms at Lammas can be intense, reflecting the bitter-sweet nature of the harvest — the joy of abundance and the acknowledgment of summer's end.

Lammas Harvest Storm Ritual:

Arrange your altar with a loaf of bread (homemade if possible) and a cup of stormwater. Break the bread and say, "I reap what I've sown, the harvest of my actions." Dip a piece of the bread into the stormwater and eat it, symbolizing the absorption of the past cycle's lessons and energies, and the nourishment for the next cycle.

Mabon (Autumn Equinox)

Mabon signifies the balance of light and dark, with the scale tipping towards the darkness. Autumn storms are characterized by steady rain and the cooling of the earth, a gradual transition into the dark half of the year.

Mabon Storm Balance Ritual:

Set up your altar with a balance scale, a bowl of rainwater, and a candle. Light the candle and say, "As the light diminishes, so the dark ascends." Place the bowl of rainwater on one side of the scale, signifying the soothing, cooling, inward energy of the Autumn rain. Take a moment to meditate on finding balance as you transition into the quieter, introspective time of the year.

Samhain

Samhain is the time when the veil between the worlds is thinnest. It is a time of honoring ancestors and preparing for the dark half of the year. Storms at this time are often chilling, stripping leaves from the trees, and ushering in the cold grip of winter.

Samhain Ancestor Storm Ritual:

Prepare your altar with photos or mementos of your ancestors, a black candle, and a vessel of stormwater. Light the candle in honor of your ancestors and say, "As the storm shakes the world, so do our ancestors shake our roots, reminding us of where we come from." Pour the stormwater into a plant or onto the earth as an offering to your ancestors.

As you weave storm symbolism and energy into your Sabbat celebrations, remember that the storm, like the Wheel of the Year, is a cycle. It has its calm and its chaos, its light and its dark, its beginnings and its endings.

By honoring the storm, you honor the cycles of nature, the cycles of life, and your own personal cycles of transformation and renewal. As the saying goes, you can't have a rainbow without a little rain. Embrace the storm, embrace the change, and watch yourself grow.

The Calm After the Storm: Integration and Reflection

One of the most powerful aspects of a storm is its inevitable end. The calm after the storm carries its own unique energy, a quiet stillness that marks the transition from chaos to tranquility. This phase is no less significant than the storm itself; in fact, it serves as a crucial period for restoration, renewal, and understanding. It's the time when we absorb the lessons of the tempest and find our footing on fresh, fertile ground.

Much like the climatic phenomenon we emulate, we too require a period of calm after our storm work. The energy that pulses through us during our rituals, meditations, and spellwork can be potent, and often leaves residual ripples within our energetic field. It is essential to balance our storm work with periods of integration and reflection to fully understand and harness the power we've drawn from the storm.

The Importance of Integration

Integration is the process of assimilating an experience into our being. It involves fully understanding the effects of our storm work on our mental, emotional, and spiritual levels. When we perform storm rituals, we channel raw, untamed energy. The vibrant force of the storm can be transformational, but it is often chaotic and can leave us feeling overwhelmed if not properly integrated.

This unstructured energy needs to be sorted, analyzed, and synthesized into a form that can benefit us. That's where integration comes in. By taking time to pause, we allow ourselves to process our experiences, anchor our insights, and ground the energy within us. This approach is essential for our spiritual health and growth.

The Power of Reflection

Reflection, on the other hand, involves consciously examining our experiences. It's an intentional act where we probe into our feelings, thoughts, and actions to derive meaning and understanding. Reflection lets us capture the essence of our storm work, documenting our journey, and ensuring we don't lose sight of the valuable lessons storms can teach us.

It helps us gain self-awareness, understand our progress, and discover areas that need more attention or development. With reflection, we become better equipped to navigate our spiritual path, refining our practices and rituals according to our unique needs and aspirations.

Post-Ritual Integration Meditation

One of the best ways to facilitate integration after your storm work is through meditation. Let's embark on a simple yet powerful meditation designed to help you integrate the storm's energy:

Find a quiet and comfortable space where you can relax undisturbed. Sit or lie down, whichever feels more comfortable.

Close your eyes and take several deep breaths. With each inhale, visualize calmness flowing into you, and with each exhale, let go of any residual tension or chaos from the storm work.

Envision yourself standing in the middle of a field, right after a storm. You can smell the fresh earth, see the dew on the grass, and hear the soft rustling of the wind.

Picture the energy of the storm as a vibrant, swirling mass within you. It could be any color or shape. Just let your intuition guide you.

Now, see this energy starting to settle down. Like the particles in a snow globe, it slowly descends and begins to spread evenly within you. Watch as the storm energy integrates into your being, becoming a part of you.

As you witness this integration, silently affirm to yourself, "I am in harmony with the storm's energy. It is a part of me, and I am a part of it."

When you feel ready, bring your awareness back to your physical surroundings. Open your eyes and sit quietly for a few moments, allowing yourself to adjust to the transformation within.

Storm Work Reflection Through Journaling

Journaling is a powerful tool for reflection. It provides a tangible record of your experiences, thoughts, and feelings, capturing your storm work journey in your own words. After every ritual or significant experience with storm energy, set aside some time to write about it.

Start by noting the basic details, like the date, the weather, and the specifics of your ritual. Then delve deeper. How did you feel before, during, and after the ritual? What thoughts and emotions arose? Did you have any revelations or surprises?

Remember, there are no right or wrong answers here. This is your journey, unique and personal. By honestly and authentically documenting your experiences, you cultivate a deeper understanding of your storm work, helping to guide and enhance your future practices.

Just as the storm is balanced by the calm that follows, our storm work must also be counterbalanced with integration and reflection. The power of the storm is transformative and potent.

By taking the time to absorb, understand, and learn from our experiences, we become not only better storm witches but more self-aware and insightful beings. As we align ourselves with the storm's cycle, we fully tap into its power for transformation and renewal.

Storm Witch's Grimoire

For a Storm Witch, one of the most sacred tools is their grimoire, or Book of Shadows. This living document serves as a storehouse of knowledge, personal experiences, and the details of magical workings. It stands as a testament to your journey, a record of your evolution and progression along the storm path. This chapter will guide you through creating and maintaining your Storm Witch's Grimoire, sharing suggested entries, layouts, and methods of recording your path.

Your grimoire should be deeply personal, reflecting your unique relationship with storms and the transformative power they hold. To that end, there's no one 'correct' way to create or maintain a grimoire. It's about finding the method that best suits you and your practice.

Choosing a Grimoire

Before you begin to record your journey, you first need to choose a vessel to hold your experiences. Your grimoire can take many forms. Some witches prefer a simple notebook, while others might choose a beautifully bound book. Still, others might favor a digital grimoire, saved on a computer or tablet.

The important thing is that your grimoire feels right to you and suits your lifestyle. If you travel often, a digital grimoire or a small, portable notebook might be best. If you love to sit at your altar with a cup of tea, a larger, beautifully bound book might serve you well. Remember, this book is a reflection of you. Let it mirror your soul and your connection to the storm.

Creating Your Grimoire

Once you've chosen your grimoire, it's time to imbue it with your energy and intention. You can do this by performing a simple consecration ritual. During a storm, if possible, sit with your grimoire and hold it in your hands. Feel the energy of the storm around you, the electricity in the air, the wind howling, and the rain pelting down. Let this energy fill you, and channel it into your grimoire.

You might want to say a small incantation or blessing, such as, "In storm's power, and with the transformative energy it holds, I consecrate this book. May it be a record of my journey, a testament to my growth, a mirror to my soul. As the storm changes the landscape, so too may my practice evolve. Blessed be."

Filling Your Grimoire

The pages of your grimoire can hold anything that relates to your journey as a Storm Witch. Here are some things you might want to include:

Storm Divinations and Observations: As you grow in your practice, you'll begin to feel more in tune with the storms around you. Record your observations and any divinations you perform. Note the date, time, weather conditions, and any intuitive feelings or thoughts you have. Over time, patterns may emerge that deepen your understanding of your connection to the storm.

Storm Rituals: Write down any rituals you perform, from simple elemental invocations to complex rites of passage. Include the date, your intention, what you did, what you felt during the ritual, and any results that manifest. This can help you refine your rituals over time and recognize what works best for you.

Deity Communications: If you work with storm-associated deities, record any communications or experiences you have with them. You may want to dedicate a section to each deity you work with, including any offerings you make and any signs or messages you receive.

Personal Reflections: Your grimoire can also serve as a journal of your spiritual journey. Write about your experiences, your feelings, and your growth. Record your doubts, your triumphs, and your revelations. Let your grimoire bear witness to your evolution as a Storm Witch.

Magical Recipes: You might want to include recipes for storm water, rituals for charging tools during a storm, or methods of harnessing storm energy. Over time, you'll develop a collection of storm-related correspondences and recipes that are unique to you.

Organizing Your Grimoire

The layout of your grimoire will depend on your personal preferences. Some witches prefer to dedicate one section to each topic, while others might organize their grimoire chronologically. Yet others might have a more fluid, intuitive organization, letting each entry flow into the next as it comes.

One way to keep your grimoire organized, no matter how you choose to arrange it, is by creating an index at the beginning or end of the book. Every time you add an entry, note the topic and page number in the index. This will make it easy to find information when you need it.

Maintaining Your Grimoire

Your grimoire is a living document, always growing and changing as you do. Don't feel you need to fill it up all at once, and don't stress over making it 'perfect.' It's a reflection of you and your practice, and like both of those things, it's meant to be a work in progress.

Regularly updating your grimoire helps keep your practice fresh and your connection to the storm strong. You might set aside time each week or after each storm to record your experiences and thoughts.

Ultimately, your Storm Witch's Grimoire is a testament to your journey. Let it be as wild, beautiful, and powerful as the storms you harness. Each entry, each page, is a step on your path, a drop of rain in the tempest of your practice. Cherish it, learn from it, and let it guide you as you navigate the transformative power of the storm.

Becoming the Eye of the Storm: Embodying Balance

Storms are a paradoxical embodiment of violent turbulence and tranquil stillness, coexisting in a delicate balance. The swirling winds, booming thunder, and brilliant lightning find their counterbalance in the eye of the storm, where an eerie calm prevails. This paradox reflects our own human existence, with our lives often caught in the whirlwind of external chaos and the inner sanctuary of peace and serenity.

The eye of the storm is not devoid of the storm; rather, it is a part of it, calmly observing and unshaken by the surrounding tempest. By learning to embody the eye of the storm, we become capable of acknowledging our emotional and life turmoil without losing our equilibrium. This chapter explores this concept, offering meditation and ritualistic practices designed to help you cultivate balance and peace amid life's tempests.

Balancing Storm Meditation

Meditation is a powerful tool to cultivate inner peace and balance. Here is a guided meditation that draws on storm imagery to help you become the eye of the storm in your own life.

Find a quiet, comfortable space where you can sit undisturbed for a while. Close your eyes and take a few deep, cleansing breaths, inhaling peace and exhaling tension.

Visualize yourself standing on a wide, open plain. Above you, storm clouds gather, their dark forms roiling and turbulent. Lightning forks down from the sky, accompanied by the roar of thunder. Rain begins to fall, carried on the gusting wind. But you are unafraid. You feel connected to this storm, a part of it.

Now, see yourself rising up into the storm, pulled into its chaotic heart. You're surrounded by the whirlwind, yet you feel no fear. The storm is a part of you, and you are a part of it.

Gradually, you find yourself drawn toward the storm's center—the eye. As you approach, the chaos subsides, and you find yourself in a place of profound calm and silence. You're in the eye of the storm, that peaceful center amidst the swirling turmoil.

Take a moment to bask in this tranquility. This is your inner sanctuary, unswayed by the surrounding tempest. No matter what rages outside, this inner calm remains untouched and inviolate.

Stay in this space as long as you need, drawing strength and peace from it. When you're ready, slowly descend from the eye, returning to your physical surroundings, carrying the serene energy of the eye of the storm with you.

Embodying Storm Energy Ritual

This ritual is designed to help you harness and embody the balancing energy of the storm, enabling you to maintain equilibrium in the midst of life's tumult.

Materials: A bowl of water, a feather, a piece of clear quartz, a candle (preferably grey or white), and an image or symbol of a storm.

Begin by cleansing your space and grounding yourself. You might want to cast a circle or call upon protective energies that align with your personal practice.

Light the candle and say, "As I light this flame, may the light of balance and calm illuminate my path."

Hold the bowl of water in your hands. Visualize the water as the rains of the storm, chaotic yet cleansing. Say, "Waters of the storm, lend me your fluidity to adapt to life's challenges."

Next, pick up the feather. This represents the winds of the storm. Say, "Winds of the storm, grant me your strength to withstand life's tempests."

Take the clear quartz and hold it aloft. The quartz symbolizes the energy of lightning, swift and illuminating. Say, "Lightning of the storm, provide me clarity amid confusion and chaos."

Lastly, hold your storm symbol or image. As you hold it, visualize yourself standing firm in the eye of the storm. Say, "I am the eye of the storm.

Around me, life may rage, but within me is a calm and tranquil center. I hold the balance, the quiet amidst the tempest. I embody the storm's power and the storm's peace."

Spend a few moments in quiet contemplation, feeling the energy of the storm within you and around you. Feel the balance of chaos and calm within you. When you're ready, thank the storm's energy, extinguish the candle, and close the circle or space in your preferred way.

Remember, embodying the eye of the storm isn't about avoiding life's chaos or suppressing your emotions. Instead, it's about finding balance within that chaos and honoring all parts of your experiences. Just as the storm embodies both turbulence and tranquility, so too can you learn to hold space for the full spectrum of your human experience—every tempest and every moment of calm. As you practice these exercises and rituals, may you find your balance, becoming your own eye of the storm.

Living as a Storm Witch: Carrying the Storm with You

Your journey with the storm does not conclude at the end of this book. Just as the tempest leaves its mark on the land, so should the Storm Witch's connection with the storm carry into every aspect of her life. It is not only about rituals and spells; it's about a unique relationship with the natural world that becomes an integral part of daily existence.

Living as a Storm Witch means carrying the storm with you always. It means being open to the energy of transformation and renewal that storms symbolize. It means respecting the destructive power of the storm, even as you embrace its capacity for change. It means seeing the beauty in the dark clouds and hearing the music in the thunder.

Carrying the Storm

Bringing the storm into your everyday life can be a conscious act. You can carry physical reminders of the storm's power, like a pendant made from a piece of lightning-struck wood or a vial of rainwater collected during a powerful storm. Symbols of storm deities can also serve as reminders and connections. A pendant of Thor's hammer, a charm representing Raijin's drums— these symbols remind us of the storm's power and our connection to it.

Integrating storm energy into your daily routines can also help you stay connected. A morning meditation visualizing yourself as a tree in a storm, your roots deep in the ground, your branches swaying with the wind, can start your day with a sense of grounded flexibility. An evening practice of journaling about your day, using the symbolism of the storm to explore your emotional landscape, can help you process your experiences.

Building a Storm Witch Community

The journey of a Storm Witch can be solitary, but it does not have to be. Storms often bring communities together, as people help each other in the aftermath. Similarly, connecting with other storm witches can provide a support network, a sounding board for ideas, and a pool of shared wisdom. Social media can be a powerful tool for building this community. Look for groups that focus on storm witchery or weather magic, or consider starting your own. Sharing experiences, insights, and questions with like-minded individuals can deepen your practice and remind you that you are not alone in your connection to the storm.

In-person gatherings, when possible, can also strengthen the storm witch community. These can be as simple as a picnic in the park on a stormy day or as elaborate as a weekend retreat dedicated to storm magic. In-person gatherings can also provide opportunities for group rituals and shared experiences that can powerfully connect you to both the storm and your fellow storm witches.

Passing On Storm Witch Traditions

As you grow in your storm witchery, you may find yourself in a position to mentor others. This can be an informal process, as you answer questions and offer advice in community groups, or it can be a more formal teacher-student relationship. Either way, sharing your knowledge and experiences can help ensure the survival and growth of storm witch traditions.

Teaching others is also a powerful way to deepen your own understanding. As you explain concepts and practices to others, you may find new insights and connections. And your students will undoubtedly teach you as well, with their questions, their unique perspectives, and their experiences.

Daily Storm Affirmation Practice

Daily affirmations can help you stay focused and connected to the storm. They can be simple statements of intent or more complex mantras that incorporate storm symbolism. Here's a simple daily storm affirmation practice to get you started:

Stand or sit comfortably, with your feet on the ground. Close your eyes and take a few deep breaths, grounding and centering yourself.

Visualize a storm building within you. See the dark clouds, feel the wind, hear the thunder. Feel the power of the storm in your heartbeat and your breath.

Speak your affirmation. This could be as simple as "I carry the storm within me," or as complex as "I am the storm, the wind of change, the thunder of transformation, the rain of renewal."

Hold the storm energy within you for a moment, then visualize it dispersing, leaving you filled with calm and power.

Repeat this practice daily, ideally at the same time each day to establish a routine.

Ritual for Blessing a Storm Witch Gathering

Whether it's a casual meetup or a formal ritual, gathering with other storm witches is a powerful experience. This ritual can help set the tone for the gathering and connect all participants to the energy of the storm:

As each person arrives, have them stand at the edge of the gathering space and call on the storm:

"Storms of the east, of air and wind, join us.
Storms of the south, of fire and lightning, join us.
Storms of the west, of water and rain, join us.
Storms of the north, of earth and ice, join us."

Once everyone has arrived and called the storm, stand in a circle. Hold hands or simply feel the energy connecting you.

One person should speak a blessing for the gathering: "We gather under the stormy sky, united by the storm's power. May our gathering be blessed with the storm's energy, its capacity for transformation, its power of renewal. May we be the storm, and may the storm be us."

Spend a moment in silence, feeling the storm energy swirling around and within the circle.

Conclude the ritual with a shared affirmation: "We are the storm."

Proceed with your gathering, carrying the storm's energy with you.

Living as a Storm Witch is a journey of connection and transformation. As you carry the storm with you, build your storm witch community, and pass on storm witch traditions, you embody the storm's power.

The storm is not just a force of nature; it is a way of life, a path to transformation and renewal. Carry the storm with you, and let it shape you as it shapes the world.

Made in the USA
Monee, IL
24 January 2025

10858412R10066